D1550249

To Andrew Carnie

7th / April / 2017

The Yellow Book

jovis

© 2016 by jovis Verlag GmbH
Texts by kind permission of the authors.
Pictures by kind permission of the photographers/holders of the
picture rights.

Editors: Thomas Sherman, Greg Logan

Photographs: Tezuka Architects (except pp. 42–48, 66–70, 73,
76–77, 80, 98–99 © Katsuhisa Kida (Fototeca); pp. 106 © Greg
Logan; pp. 146–147 © Thomas Sherman)

Design and setting: Thomas Sherman, Greg Logan
Proofreading: Justin Ross, Berlin
Printing and binding: Graspo CZ, a. s., Zlín

Bibliographic information published by the Deutsche
Nationalbibliothek
The Deutsche Nationalbibliothek lists this publication in the
Deutsche Nationalbibliografie; detailed bibliographic data are
available on the Internet at http://dnb.d-nb.de

jovis Verlag GmbH
Kurfürstenstrasse 15/16
10785 Berlin

www.jovis.de

jovis books are available worldwide in selected bookstores.
Please contact your nearest bookseller or visit www.jovis.de for
information concerning your local distribution.

ISBN 978-3-86859-423-2

Tezuka Architects:
The Yellow Book
Edited by Thomas Sherman & Greg Logan

jovis

Contents

Acknowledgments

The Yellow Book began in a conversation between Takaharu Tezuka and Tom Sherman in March of 2015. Tom had come to visit the Tezuka office as part of a larger research project on timber architecture. During the visit, Tezuka—who was excited about transforming his 2013 lecture at the Harvard Graduate School of Design (GSD) into a standalone publication—asked Tom to edit the volume. Later that year Greg Logan, who had previously worked at Tezuka Architects and was in Tokyo conducting research of his own, came to visit the office. At that time it was proposed that an interview could complement the lecture and add depth to the overall publication. These two texts form the backbone of *The Yellow Book:* the lecture, which functions as a set of stories that detail Tezuka Architects most salient projects; and the interview, which investigates how Tezuka developed his design philosophy and how this translates to the office's built work.

While every effort was made to preserve the original intent and tone of both the lecture and interview, a number of editorial decisions were made in the interest of adapting these more casual, spoken pieces to the more formally specific demands of a printed text targeted toward an international, English-speaking audience. Dialect and vocabulary were carefully curated to be both true to the author's voice and easy for the reader to follow. In rare instances, passages have been trimmed or reordered in the interest of global continuity and logical linear progression within the text. Finally, Japanese names have been rendered in the Western style of given name followed by family name.

The title of this book is taken from the role color plays in the Tezuka family and office symbology. Yellow is the color of all that is shared and communal for the Tezukas—from their car all the way down to condiments in the fridge. Thus, we decided on the title *The Yellow Book* because we see the book as a collection of shared thoughts and philosophies that bind not only the Tezuka family and the Tezuka office together, but also the Tezukas to their shared place in society. *The Yellow Book* is, therefore, an explication on how the Tezukas believe they fit into this world and what role they believe their architecture can play in it.

The Yellow Book would not have been possible without the generous help of a great number of people. We would like to thank Dean Mohsen Mostafavi and Professor Mark Mulligan (both from the GSD) for their contributions to the text as well as the generous contribution of their time and feedback. Philipp Sperrle and Susanne Roesler of JOVIS Verlag were instrumental in providing their publishing expertise in helping to make the book a reality. Special thanks must be given to Midori Taki, Sockkee Ooi, and Aurapim Phongsirivech of Tezuka Architects for their tireless efforts in facilitating communications between the office and us, as well as providing invaluable editing and design feedback. Finally, our deepest thanks to Takaharu and Yui Tezuka for opening their office to us to share their insights on design and the architect's role in society.

Foreword

Mohsen Mostafavi
Dean
Alexander and Victoria Wiley Professor of Design
Harvard Graduate School of Design

Japan's urban architecture is often reticent, perhaps too reticent. Of course, this does not prevent Japanese cities from being exciting places to live and work; the necessary intensity is generated by other things—the people, the culture, the food. And yet, at the same time, the anonymity of the urban landscape has served as a foil for some of the most refined, sophisticated, well-built, and seductive buildings to be found anywhere in the world.

Much of this work can be defined by its adherence to simplicity. Like a really good sashimi, Japanese architecture is often about distilling things to their pure essence, with the emphasis being on subtraction, rather than addition. In many respects, the work of Tezuka Architects is within this genealogy, yet it is unique in its own way—and often far removed from the projects that are produced within the implicit circles of architects such as Toyo Ito or Sanaa.

More than anything else, the work of Tezuka Architects is defined by its sense of pleasure—a pleasure that extends equally to the making of the project and to its reception by the users. There is also a lightness of touch. Tezuka Architects try to design buildings that are not just open to nature, but allow nature to enter inside—sometimes literally, as when they incorporate existing trees into an interior. "You are waterproof, you never melt in the rain, so children should be outside," is how Takaharu Tezuka rationalizes the nearly year-round openness to the elements of the Fuji Kindergarten, a building that seems to perfectly define the practice's approach to life and architecture.

I first met Takaharu (Tak) when he was a graduate student in a studio I taught at the University of Pennsylvania in 1989.

Even then he was very different from most of the other students. Not only focused but capable, he was committed to his way of working from the very beginning. He would make very precise white models—not just one, but many—of all his design projects. At once conceptual and buildable, these models and drawings demonstrated his incredible enthusiasm and love for architecture. Tak also attended the theory class I used to teach for the post-professional students, immersing himself in some difficult writings and engaging in discussions on the connections between theory and practice. It was good to hear recently that this class, even though quite challenging in terms of both language and ideas, was helpful for him as a teacher years later.

After graduation, Tak spent time in London working with the British architect Richard Rogers. It was there that he encountered Richard's infectious love of primary colors and of people, and had the opportunity to visit one of Richard's early projects—the groundbreaking house he designed for his parents in the suburban neighborhood of Wimbledon. Tak seems to have fallen in love with this exceptional building, which in some ways contains the DNA of Richard's later work. The Wimbledon house, with its colorful interiors, would turn out to be an important influence on the work of the practice that Tak and his partner Yui set up on their return to Japan.

For Tezuka, the building of architecture is a communal act involving the client, the users, and even the architects' family. The parents, as the principals of the firm, are part of a performance group with their son and daughter—a colorfully clad circus troupe of sorts, dedicated to the joys of architecture. For the annex to the Fuji Kindergarten, the practice designed a "classroom without furniture," a five-meter-tall building with seven levels—the clearances range from 500 to 1,500 millimeters: "When we showed our son and daughter they touched the ceiling with their hands, smiling. The principal, Mr. Kato, said that for children, the ceiling is like the sky—they cannot touch it. When the sky is lowered to their level, it transports them into the world of giant adults." The junior Tezukas were then sent to explore the safety implications of a building with low ceiling heights and many steps without guardrails. "Just as we had expected, there were a few small bumps and bruises, but nothing serious." For the Tezukas, learning to navigate these small obstacles and gain control of one's surroundings is an important part of the children's broader education: "These days kids need a small dose of danger. For on such occasions they learn to help each other. This is society." The social responsibility of the architect was another lesson instilled by Richard Rogers. As Tak puts it, "He [Richard] never talks about details, he talks about human life."

In one of those curious twists of fate, Richard Rogers recently donated the Wimbledon house to Harvard, for use as the base for a new residential fellowship program for the Graduate School of Design. Now Tak and I have something else in common to appreciate. Life is strange—and in a good way too.

Introduction

Mark Mulligan
Associate Professor in Practice of Architecture
Harvard Graduate School of Design

The idea for this book originated in a lecture that Takaharu Tezuka gave at Harvard's Graduate School of Design (GSD) in October 2013.

It was not the first time he had spoken at the GSD; ten years earlier, at a time when their practice was just beginning to attract international attention, he and Yui Tezuka had presented their work here at a "Tokyo Micro-Urbanism" conference. Amid a lineup of exciting young presenters—who today represent some of the most innovative practices in Japan—the Tezukas stood out not only for the sheer number of projects that their small practice had completed in its first eight years, but also for the provocative yet approachable tone set by Takaharu. From the start of our friendship, what impressed me most about this blue-shirted architect was his gift for storytelling.

Of course, one could argue that elaborate narratives are not required to appreciate the appeal of this architecture. Precisely composed and photogenic, the Tezukas' projects have been widely published in Japan and around the world. The architecture is particularly remarkable for its mutability: its ability to take on different appearances depending on the season, the time of day, and the activities taking place there. Buildings respond freely to exterior conditions and occupants' wishes, typically by varying the degree of closure or openness to a surrounding exterior space. In aiming to heighten qualities of architectural mutability, the work is tied into a long tradition of Japanese vernacular architecture known for its sliding doors, screens, and other boundary-modulating elements. Spatial fluidity and interior-exterior continuity today might be considered universal tropes of modern architecture; still, when we see how far the Tezukas will go in opening their architecture to life-giving elements of sunlight, wind, and humidity—creating the impression of "boundary-free" living—there is an undeniable, tangible freshness in the work. Their modestly scaled, immodestly open houses seem well suited to citizens of the twenty-first century, overlaying a post-materialist, ubiquitous Wi-Fi lifestyle with a return to nature.

This much is immediately clear in published photographs; yet our appreciation of these projects grows undeniably richer in the author's storytelling. Tezuka has a seemingly innate ability to capture his audience's attention and bring them to the heart of a topic or idea, however tangentially he may get there. His uniquely spontaneous and interactive speaking style draws people into his world, and in his hands seemingly off-topic anecdotes become vehicles for sharing the kinds of personal thoughts, observations, and doubts about contemporary urban life that rarely get aired in formal presentations of new architecture. Projects are never presented as the result of fixed ideas; their design evolves along with the architects' personal relationships with their clients and collaborators; architecture becomes a medium for connecting with an interesting and diverse universe of personalities. And the post-occupancy stories of these projects—in what might be termed their "post-partum" phase—turn out to be as interesting and instructive as their creation stories. Architecture ultimately shapes, and becomes a setting for, continuously unfolding human events.

Tezuka's narrative gift was fully evident when he returned to the GSD in 2013, speaking in Piper Auditorium to a packed audience of students and faculty. In the intervening decade since his first visit, the firm's commissions had diversified, and the portfolio had grown to include more than one hundred completed works. Yet, that evening Tezuka avoided using his speaker's platform merely to promote the dozens of new works they'd produced; in fact, only a small number were presented. His talk focused on a set of philosophical positions on architecture that could be illustrated with a balanced mix of early and new works. In describing the experience of working with the 2001 Roof House's unconventional clients, Tezuka re-enacted memorable moments of the project development with child-like amazement and perfect comedic timing. Presenting important recent projects like the Fuji Kindergarten (2007), Asahi Kindergarten (2012), and Child Chemo House (2013) elicited from the architect new and deeper reflections on architecture's relationship to fundamental human psychology. Throughout the lecture, amid the high spirits and laughter, serious themes emerged—about professional responsibilities, about maintaining a humble and open attitude in creative work—and provoked a lively Q&A session.

The evening made a deep impression on many students, and *The Yellow Book* is a novel attempt to capture and extend the spirit of the event. Transforming the narration of a slide lecture, including many spontaneous remarks, into a written text requires not only careful transcription and text editing but also a clear curatorial overview. In the process, the editors are hoping to further distill the lessons of Tezuka's project experiences and experiments so that students and young professionals might use *The Yellow Book* as a non-technical pocket manual to encourage and inspire their future work.

Sketch of the Roof House

Beyond Architecture

Lecture by Takaharu Tezuka
Harvard Graduate School of Design (GSD)
Cambridge, Massachusetts
October 8, 2013

Good evening. Other than faculty members, is there anyone here from my lecture four years ago? No one? Great! Then at least I can make some of the same jokes again! I first came to speak here ten years ago, and at that time Toshiko Mori was the chair. I was eager to show our studio's work to Professor Mori that evening, but my daughter, who was only five months old at the time, started to cry during the lecture. Professor Mori nicely carried her out of the room, but unfortunately she didn't end up hearing much of anything from my lecture. I guess the talk went well though because I am now back here at Harvard for my third lecture.

I'd like to tell you another quick story about another member of the GSD faculty.

Many years ago, when I was a student at the University of Pennsylvania, I took a class from Mohsen Mostafavi. At the time my English was very bad, so I only understood about twenty-five percent of his lectures. Determined to learn, I kept reading and rereading the texts that he assigned, and now I am teaching a class on architectural theory in Japan and I am using some of the very same material that had caused me so much difficulty!

So let's start with some basics, like how to recognize me. I am always in blue: my shirt, my iPhone, and my wallet are all blue. Everybody jokes that I am always wearing the same blue T-shirt, but actually I have more than one hundred of them, so I assure you that this one is quite clean. My wife Yui is always in red. One day we decided that everything we shared should be yellow, so when we had our daughter, we also decided to make her yellow. When we had a son we were going to make him yellow as well, but our daughter didn't want to lose her color, so she made him green.

Our other family is, of course, our office. In that respect, our office is quite different from most architecture offices in Japan. In Japan everybody works long hours, starting at 8am and often working until midnight or later. But in our office, if somebody says to me, "I want to go on a date with my boyfriend or girlfriend," I let them go. One of the things that I am very proud of in our office is that there have been six marriages in the last two years. Lately, there has even been some procreation going on, so I feel a bit like a grandfather these days.

I always say, "If you don't know happiness, how can you provide happiness to others?" This is a very important saying in our office. With that in mind, I would like to start with the smallest and cheapest project we have ever done. In an effort to get to know our clients as close friends, we always ask them before we start a new project, "How do you like to spend your weekends?" and "What kind of things do you like to eat?"

Clients as Allies

Several years ago, we designed a house for a family who told us that they usually spend their time on the roof of their small house. They took us to a small window and jumped out. At the time I couldn't believe it, but then they showed me this photo of their children on the roof. This would, no doubt, be illegal in the United States (US). There are no handrails and two of the roof tiles are even falling off. I told them that it looked quite dangerous, but they said, "Don't worry, we go out with them all the time." I wasn't sure if it was okay, but at least I knew they were serious.

So we made a simple drawing. The house we designed had an inclined roof that looked down the valley to a holy mountain. Whenever we talk about this project with our students, we tell them to never go to McDonald's on a first date. If you're sitting at a small table at McDonald's, talking with your date, you might chat for thirty minutes or so. But after thirty minutes, you will run out of things to talk about. Then silence comes, which is very awkward, so you start saying the wrong things. That is how things go bad. I should mention that I once made the mistake of making this point at a lecture where McDonald's was the sponsor of the lecture!

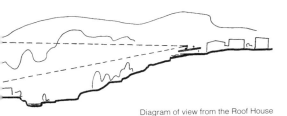

Diagram of view from the Roof House

Anyhow, there is a river close to the university where I teach called the Tama River. Along the beautiful riverbank, we always see couples sitting there, and we wanted to know why this was the case. We reasoned that if you are sitting on a sloping site you aren't looking directly at each other, because you are sitting on the slope facing the same direction. When you aren't facing each other silence isn't as awkward. It can actually be quite romantic. Secondly, since you are looking at the same thing you are sharing the same view. You might say, "Did you see that splash in the water? There is probably a fish down there." This kind of stupid conversation never works at McDonald's. In the end, a sloping site makes it easier to move onto the next stage of a relationship, but I don't need to talk about the details of this.

We researched squares around the world, and I found that most of the popular squares for gathering are inclined, like the one in front of the Pompidou Center, in Sienna, in Melbourne, or in the Piazza San Marco in Venice. If you look at photos of the

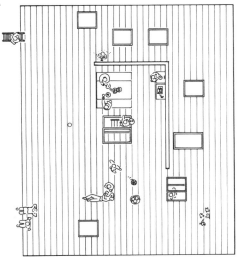

Top: Couple sitting on the roof
Bottom: Roof plan of Roof House

Piazza San Marco, you will see people on the edge of the Piazza and only pigeons in the middle. In the end, we realized the importance of an inclined plane and we decided to make the slope of the Roof House the same as the inclination of the ground.

Since they were used to jumping from a window, the family told us that it was boring to use a door to get outside. I'm sure you know the feeling: when you do something you are not supposed to do, you feel strangely good. So we decided to put a skylight in the children's bedroom. The elder sister said, "This skylight is mine," while the father said, "The one from the bedroom belongs to me," and the mother said, "This one in the kitchen is mine." Eventually we ended up with 8 skylights, including ones for the toilet and the bathroom.

The family had a number of requests for the roof that drove our design process. They wanted to be able to have breakfast and lunch on the roof, so we designed a table with benches. They wanted to be able to cook, so we added a kitchen. They told us, "The winter is very cold, so we have to have a stove, and in summer it is very hot, so we need to have a shower," so these were added as well. They even went so far as to ask for a barbecue on top of the house, but I told them that I didn't think it was a good idea. I told them that it was a timber house and that they were going to burn it down!

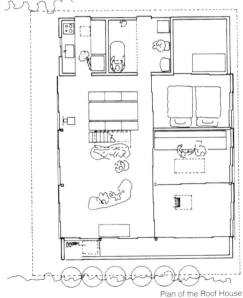

Plan of the Roof House

They said, "Okay. We can have a barbecue in the garden, but you have to make sure the roof is low enough to pass food up to the roof." So we made the ceiling height only 1.9 meters, but this is high enough for a Japanese person, although maybe not for an American.

The wife then said, "My mother lives about eighty meters down that way, and she opens her windows every morning. I want to have a view to her house to make sure that she is okay." So we cut the corner away

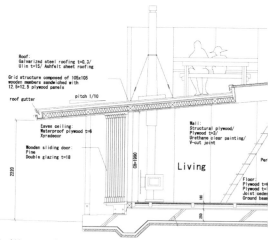

Roof House section

from the wall. Actually, this wall was the only thing giving them privacy. They are a very strange family. Imagine them sitting on top of the roof!

Once, while we were there during construction, the clients ordered pizza. The delivery boy came, but since he couldn't find anyone he called back to the restaurant and asked, "Where are they? Who ordered pizza?" They told him, "They're on the roof! Look for a ladder around the corner." When he made it to the top of the ladder,

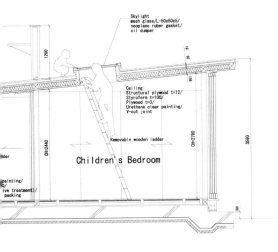

the first thing he said was, "Where do I take off my shoes?"[1] This pleased the family so much that they kept ordering pizza from the rooftop! They used to always have the same person deliver the pizza, but one day the boy never came back. From then on a different delivery person came each time they ordered a pizza. So they asked, "What happened to the boy who used to always deliver our pizza?" The deliveryman said, "You know, this house has become so famous at Pizza Hut that now we take turns so that everyone can come and see the house." The Roof House had become the most famous house in the entire region for the local Pizza Hut!

The two neighbors who live close by were also very happy. The Roof House used to be a two-story building, but now it's a single story house and it feels as if they have an outdoor deck in front of their home. The guy living right next door always offers us a beer when we visit, and if we accept he

---

1. Traditionally, in the Japanese home, a *genkan* is a lowered entry area for removing shoes before stepping into the family's living space. The delivery person considered the roof a part of the home, signifying the importance of the roof to the family.

comes over and drinks the beer on the roof with us. The small street in front of the house used to always be empty, but now every morning there are people out stretching their legs and walking their dogs because it has become a custom to say good morning to the family while they are having breakfast on the roof. Eventually, the husband became the representative of his town, so our architecture can work for elections.

When we completed the project, it was published in all sorts of magazines; we have counted up to 400 citations from around the world, and it's still ongoing. The chief editor of *Architecture Review* told us that this was the most published house worldwide in the last ten years. But then complaints starting coming in. Although the Roof House was on the front cover of many magazines, some people still said that it should be illegal without handrails. In fact, the owner of the Roof House is a trained architect; he has a license and can stamp planning application drawings for approval. He said, "You know, we used to live in a normal house, and it had no handrails on the roof. If you look around the neighborhood, no house has handrails, or if you look down the valley, no house down there has handrails either. So why should we have to have a handrail on top of my house?" This is how he convinced me, and as you can see we got the approval from the planning application authority.

We believe that architecture is for people. That is why we always show people in our drawings. In the roof plan, the elder sister is playing soccer and the younger sister is sitting on the edge, someone is showering, and another is having a meal near the kitchen. And for the first time in the history of the magazine *Japan Architect*, they published a photo with people in it.

View to the valley

Usually, Japanese architecture magazines are so serious and do not include people in their photos. In our work, people are often smiling and the Japanese architecture magazines don't like that. In fact, in the very next issue, a critic wrote, "This architecture is not realistic; the rooftop is undoubtedly very hot in summer and very cold in winter. I don't think the rooftop is in use. The picture is likely a fiction." For the first time in the ninety-year history of the magazine, the client wrote back to *Japan Architect*, saying, "It's not a fiction! We eat breakfast on the roof everyday!"

Perhaps because this house received a number of prizes from the government and the Japan Institute of Architects (JIA), a younger generation of architects started to draw people on top of their buildings. However, their planning applications would always be denied. The authorities would always tell them "No, you have to have a handrail!" But the young architects would say, "Do you know this project? It's an award-winning building!" And they would show them a picture of the Roof House.

Of course, the building authority would always say that they knew the project and that it was exactly the reason they couldn't do it anymore. So the Roof House was the first project without a handrail on the roof, and also the last project. Nobody can do it anymore. We like this fact very much.

When the project ended up winning the *Japan Architect* magazine prize, the client made a speech saying, "The rooftop is very hot in the summer, so you should use it before sunrise. And the rooftop is very cold in the winter, so you should use it after lunchtime after it has had time to warm up." I think that this was a very wise statement. He said, "In summer, we might go to a beach where it's very hot, even

Dining on the roof

hotter than anywhere in the city. In the winter we might go skiing, where it's –20 degrees Celsius, but as long as we are having fun we can live with it. We are not the kind of people to search for the most comfortable temperature; we search for the fun in life."

Even after getting to know the family, we were surprised by their commitment to life on the roof. This roof has the worst kitchen I have ever designed! We didn't have any money, so we asked the carpenter to bring whatever materials he had available. This sink came from his backyard, but they use it quite often. We were not sure if they were going to actually use the roof shower—we thought that maybe the daughter who was eight years old might use it—but then we

Interior of the Roof House

got a call from the wife saying; "it's very nice to take a warm shower in a cold typhoon."

"Oh my goodness," I said, "you have to be very careful."

But she said, "I'm okay, because I always wear a T-shirt." I don't think she understood what I was concerned about. My point is that the family is actually using the roof all the time.

There is no privacy in the house, but sliding doors come out to divide the space, and as you can see there are no paper screens or curtains. The bathroom and shower are on one side, but the bedroom is on the other side, so we asked them how they get to their bedroom after they take a shower. They replied, "don't worry, we are fast runners, so nobody can see us." They admire the American life, but I don't think they understand that the distance from the street to the house is different in the US.

You know this was fourteen years ago, and because this project had such a low budget we could only afford to make one kind of structural beam section. The beams are about one hundred millimeters (four inches) square. They are very small members and we put plywood on both sides. Actually, this was a good way to make the roof thin but strong. If the roof is thin like a sheet of paper, you can pop your head up through the skylight and experience two worlds juxtaposed on either side of that sheet of paper. You can tell how important it was to make the roof very thin when you see the photo with the red and blue couple sitting on the edge of the roof and see two pairs of socks dangling down. It's a very simple diagram.

We always work with our lighting designer, and he told me a very good story: "Do you know the most beautiful lighting scheme in the world? It is a night view of the city. It's beautiful not because of the color or arrangement, but because you feel the life behind each light. When you see a red or yellow light, this might be lighting an Indian woman making curry for her grandchild. If you see a white light moving by quickly, it might be a couple going somewhere. If you see a bright light in a building, it could be somebody working late. You can feel the lives behind the lights." He conducted an interesting experiment in the city of Yokohama. The city asked him to make a street in the Motomachi district brighter because it used to be a famous gathering spot for people. The project was supposed to take a few years and had a budget of a few million dollars per year, but he came

Nighttime at the Roof House

back within a few months saying that he had finished the task. As promised, the street had become much brighter than before, and the city council members asked him, "What did you do?" He replied, "It was simple. I turned off the streetlights." You might be surprised to hear this. However, the eye is an incredible device that can adjust to the brightness of light. Sunlight is 10,000 lux, but we can see things even at one lux. Before, the city kept improving the strength of the streetlights, each time making them brighter and brighter, while the shop lights stayed at around 300 lux. This created a very bright street but drowned out the shop lights on the side. When he turned off the streetlights, life came back to the street and it became beautiful again. That was what he told us when he convinced me to use the light bulbs dangling down in the Roof House. It works quite well. It appears lively from the outside, and each skylight has its own lantern. It's a one-to-one relationship; each space has one light bulb dangling down, each skylight has one ladder, and each skylight has an owner.

This house taught me two very important lessons. First, a concept does not require an explanation. Usually, students want to explain a concept for ten or twenty minutes, but a professor will typically stop them and tell them that their explanation is boring. This house was published throughout the world, but we never needed to send a text to the publishers because they knew what was going on; it was easy enough to understand the project through the pictures. Second, we found that architecture can change lives. The client's wife has a degree in psychology, and she worked as a professional counselor at the

The Roof House at night

local junior high school. She found that the counseling sessions were not going well in the concrete building, so she started to bring the students to the Roof House. One student was acting like a tough guy, but as soon as he came up to the rooftop he changed his attitude and said, "I would be a better man if I had grown up on top of this roof." Now, he is over thirty years old, went to a good university, and is a representative of what we call "the Roof House Foundation."

Re-Imagining Program

After completing the Roof House, we had a client tell us, "We want a Roof House for 600 children." The existing school was one of the ugliest buildings I had ever seen, but for some reason I liked the feeling of it. I said, "You should keep it. It feels good to me." But the principal disagreed, and he took me around to see all the roof leaks. There were more than thirty in total. The principal convinced me that this school wouldn't stand through the next earthquake, and I finally agreed that a new building was the right decision. So we had to do something.

As I have said, we have two kids, yellow and green, and we know that they love running in circles. When we brought them to the site, they kept making circles around the chairs. It is as if they had a primitive need to do this, like a puppy that tries to bite its own tail by running in circles. So we designed the school to also be in the form of a circle so that the children could keep running, never knowing when to stop. Also, there used to be several buildings along the street, and the principal used to make rounds through them. I liked that situation so we also made

Diagram of view to the roof at Fuji Kindergarten

the school circular for him, so that he also
never knows when to stop!

However, when we pushed the circle
to the perimeter of the site, it interfered with
the location of the existing trees. It's not
easy to keep trees alive within a building.
You can't cut the roots. If you do, the tree
dies. So, we located the roots using sonar,
and developed a grid of steel beams to
work around the trees, while also keeping
the roof thin. While we were designing,
the principal told us, "We don't want any
handrails like the Roof House," but I told him
that it was impossible and if we did that at
a kindergarten someone would surely sue
us. He came back to us and asked, "How

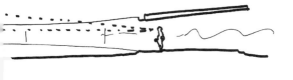

about nets sticking out from the edges so we can catch the children falling off?" He was serious! But eventually he convinced me, and we went to the planning application department of the city to explain the idea. They said, "Are you insane?" So I went back to the principal, telling him they thought I was crazy. The principal then called the city department, and talked to a guy whose child was actually going to this kindergarten. The city officials also knew the kindergarten well because everybody from the area had children going there. The principal is much more famous than the local mayor, so the city planning department had to do something.

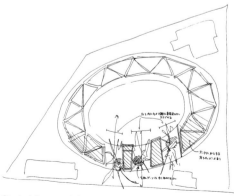

Steel reinforcement diagram

Eventually, they gave us permission to keep the net idea but only around the trees that come up through the building. We were allowed to call this net a "handrail," and, like the Roof House, because we did it first the younger generation can't do it anymore.

As you can guess, the kids love to climb and fall into the net. Sometimes there are more than forty kids climbing the trees at the same time. Since the principal never wanted a handrail on the edge of the roof, when we made a few mock-ups, he went to the weakest handrail and said, "I like this shaky one." So we ended up with a very elegant but very shaky handrail, which I am sure is illegal in the US. But it looks great from underneath, and the children look like monkeys at the zoo.

The building has a very low ceiling height of 2.1 meters, about seven feet. There is a governmental recommendation or code, which says the ceiling height must be three meters (ten feet) for schools, but the principal didn't agree with this. He wanted the ceiling to be low so that he could see what was happening on the roof. The kids are very small, so we also didn't want any high ceilings for their sake. However, the local government authority and Ministry of Education complained about it, but the principal said, "this is private school and is paid for with private funds," so we were able to keep the low ceilings in the end.

But about two and a half years ago, the authorities began to change their mind. The

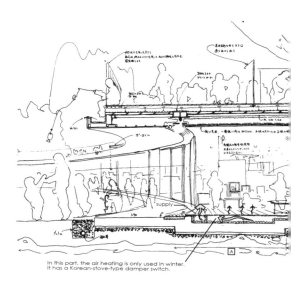

In this part, the air heating is only used in winter.
It has a Korean-stove-type damper switch.

Ministry of Education called the principal and said, "something wonderful has happened." United Nations Educational, Scientific and Cultural Organization (UNESCO) and the Organisation for Economic Co-operation and Development (OECD) had announced that they were searching worldwide for the best school building built in the last fifty years. All countries in the United Nations

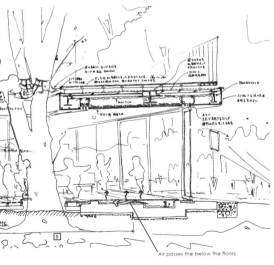

Air passes the below the floors.

Section of Fuji Kindergarten

submitted projects, but the OECD and UNESCO selected Fuji Kindergarten as the best. You know, the Japanese government rarely listens to the people of Japan, but they listen to the US and Europe. So they changed their minds about the kindergarten after an international body like UNESCO had noticed it. They came to Fuji Kindergarten and awarded it a Ministry of Education Prize, the first kindergarten to be awarded such a prize in the history of the Japanese government. We went to Paris to receive the UNESCO prize, and a group of government officials ended up coming along with us. When we came back, Yui was appointed to establish new standards for kindergartens in Japan. Now we are allowed to do whatever we want! We were not supposed to allow kids on the roof, but if you look at the new government standards, we are now encouraged to do it. It's so nice to be on the side of the government. We can make our own rules now!

The building looks simple, but if you go there you'll notice that the columns are very narrow. About 7 percent of the world's active volcanoes are in Japan, and 30 percent of magnitude 4 earthquakes happen in Japan; it is an earthquake-prone country. Therefore, it is very unusual to have such small columns spaced at such distant intervals. We used advanced technology and simulation to make them thin. Each beam was engineered with different harmonics to avoid resonant frequency, even with the children running on the roof.

There are many skylights, with at least one in each room. At Christmas, Santa Claus comes down through a skylight, but four or five years ago, there was a problem. The principal really wanted a nice-looking American Santa Claus from the American military base, but he didn't realize that the skylights were made for a Japanese Santa Claus, and the American Santa got stuck in the window frame and they could not get him out!

We designed a number of details in the project specifically for the children. This mound of earth in the courtyard is there to keep the roof access stairway from being too long—otherwise the kids might get injured. This roof scupper helps them learn how rain becomes groundwater. This is the wash area, and there are variations in the water taps. There is one to spray water on friends, one to shower with, a big water tap, and in this photo here, he's not washing his boots, rather, he is putting water in his boots!

These days, people always say we should use LED lights to reduce energy usage, but we disagree. Using LED lights doesn't guarantee you will not waste energy. At Fuji Kindergarten there are over 300 individual light bulbs and more than 100 pull strings hanging from the ceiling. Therefore, when you pull on one string you

Aerial view of Fuji Kindergarten

can only turn on three lights at a time. This is a lesson for the children, to always pull the same string to turn off the lights when they leave. This is the kind of conscientiousness we are trying to teach through our design.

Fuji Kindergarten is also famous for two things. First of all, at this kindergarten there are no social outcasts in the classroom. The principal believes that when you place children in a cage they will try to establish a hierarchy, and the lowest caste gets segregated; but when you have no boundaries, there is no need to create such hierarchies. Secondly, autistic children are able to integrate with other students and rarely show their symptoms while at the school. Typical building regulations say that you need to have a box in the classroom where an autistic child can hide, but here, if a child doesn't like the class, they can move to the next classroom. They may run away, but eventually they will make their way back to where they started. The plan is circular, after all. If a student still has a problem, the teacher puts him or her on a pony and that usually solves the problem right away.

Autistic children show symptoms when they are in a concrete box where they don't hear any noise, but when they are brought into a noisy field, their symptoms often subside. A scientist I know found that this has to do with background noise, and when he provides white noise at a frequency of more than 20 kilohertz, the children no longer show symptoms. This is the kind of background noise that happens naturally at Fuji Kindergarten. The classrooms are divided by sliding doors and stacking furniture, allowing noise to travel in between the rooms. Do you know the Kecak dance from Bali? If you listen to a recording of the dance, you can you hear the beeps and buzzing of insects in the background, but when we were there, we didn't notice it at all. The Kecak dance happens in the jungle, and when you are in the jungle, you recognize the noises as part of the environment, and your brain cancels them out. That sound is about seventy decibels, equivalent to a construction site. Your cardiovascular system also produces a great deal of noise, but your brain cancels this out as well. Noise cancellation occurs not by frequency, but by information.

Another professor did research on how many games the children play on the roof, and he found that there are six times more games played here than at a typical kindergarten. There are no rules to tell the children what they should do. The architecture allows them to choose how they want to play. The professor also studied the movement of children and found that the average child at this kindergarten runs about three miles daily, which is also extremely unusual. That is eight times more

than at a normal kindergarten, but it is just their spontaneous movement. There are no toys, just ordinary architectural elements, and the rooftop is inclined just slightly towards the outside edge. The children run continuously on the roof every morning, and because of the inclination they don't feel that they will spin out. They run as fast as they want. These children have the highest scores for athletic ability in Tokyo. The professor asked, "How do you train them?" and a teacher replied, "We just leave them alone, they run by themselves."

View of classroom space and tree courtyard

We later got a new commission from the school for a bus station and two English classrooms adjacent to the first building we designed. We decided to wrap our new building around a tree, and our friend, the British architect Peter Cook, was the one who named it "Ring Around a Tree." Since there are no regulations requiring us to have a three-meter ceiling height, we designed seven floors within five meters; the ceiling height is only 1.2 meters. As I said before, we make the regulations now.

You can see the tree in the middle. The floor is very thin, and we tried to make the columns much thinner than the structure of the tree, so that the building belongs to the tree. When we design like this, we worry

Ring Around a Tree

that something dangerous might happen, so we always allow our children to test how safe it is [laughter]. My son bumped his head trying to jump off, and my daughter crawled up the tree and almost fell off the edge, so we knew we had to do something in these spots. Afterward, we let the children from the kindergarten test it. They love to touch the ceiling, because usually they can't reach the ceiling in other buildings. You can see how happy they are when they line up to jump off. Traffic is always is a problem in Tokyo! [laughter].

It's funny, when you bring children hiking on a mountain there are no handrails, but once you start building things you have to put handrails all over the place. These days, I hear of the term "Helicopter Parents," who watch over their children all the time, spoiling them. At this kindergarten, the principal made a fantastic statement: "This is a private kindergarten, and even though your kids might break an arm or leg, we'll make sure that they don't break their spirit."

Living Architecture

I want to introduce a project we designed in an area of Japan that gets some of the heaviest snowfall in the world. The Matsunoyama Natural Science Museum is a sixty-meter long Corten steel building. Interestingly, it is about twenty-six centimeters longer in the summer because of thermal expansion. The building has very thick and heavy glass windows because during the winter snow falls rapidly in this region, which gets even more snowfall than Alaska. In total, they get around thirty meters of snow per year, which compacts down to about five or six meters of ice. In a week, the snow is already more than seven meters

Matsunoyama Natural Science Museum in the snow

deep, and through the window you can see a cross section of the snow. One day, I got a call from the curator asking, "Are you sure this is okay?" "Well, we calculated the snow load," I said. They called me again, and I said, "I think it's ok …," but as the snow kept building they called once more saying, "We're getting quite worried." But, from the museum window, you can see a nice line of light through the snow. We call it the Tadao Ando effect. This museum building also brought with it a new discovery: there is a whole world happening under the snow. There are animals and insects burrowing through it at all times. It is like a kind of an aquarium.

Snow accumulation visible on the interior

The Woods of Net project was designed for a children's climbing net woven by the Canadian-Japanese artist Toshiko Horiuchi Macadam for the Open Air Museum in Hakone. The net is nearly forty years old, but because she is so famous these days, the museum asked us to design a new pavilion. Initially they wanted a white building with a tall ceiling, but I said, "No, we should leave this outside, because a spider's web looks better in the forest." They told me it couldn't be done because the volcanic activity nearby could melt the net. So we had to design a shed that could contain the net, control the wind because of the mountainous site, yet also feel like an outdoor pavilion. It was quite difficult.

Woods of Net

This is in a natural forest reserve, so we had to get special permission for the building. We built a study model, about the size of my hand, and I brought this model to the Minister of the Environment to get approval. I explained that this is architecture, but at the same time it is a kind of artwork. It is one hundred percent wood because we wanted to understand the culture of wooden construction in Japanese architecture and not use any metal joinery. They said, "Oh that's a great idea!" They approved the design, but I never told them that the model was only at 1:1000 scale. Later, they were quite upset when they saw how big the building actually was!

We then studied joinery techniques of traditional Japanese architecture, used in buildings like Kiyomizu-dera in Kyoto, which is about 700 years old. There are even some wooden buildings in Japan more than 1,000 years old. It's a very old tradition. We eventually arrived at this study model. The design for the Woods of Net looks erratic, like a random structure, but actually it is quite rational. It is a balance between the shear and the bending moment. We worked with the structural engineer Norihide Imagawa (TIS & Partners), who is also a professor, to develop a new algorithm. Professor Imagawa developed a cloud computation to make precise calculations because we had to deal with uncertainties. We made sure that each square centimeter carried the same weight, so each member has a different section and joint connection. This looks like a 3D drawing, but it's not, it's the result of the algorithm. It is a marriage between the latest technology and tradition or, as we say, it is a kind of "nostalgic future."

It fits quite well with its surroundings. It blends into the forest without imitating it. When we make things in the forest, we try to make the architecture as if it were a living form, as if it breathes. The architecture should be alive like a creature. The artist designed the net as a great place for children to play. They love to find their way around inside the net, and I think that this is also a form of architecture. We wanted our architecture to strengthen that experience.

Top: Woods of Net in construction
Bottom: Interior with woven sculpture

A Legacy of Ideas not Objects

I expect you may have seen many pictures of the tsunami in Tohoku. Following the disaster, UNICEF came to us to rebuild a kindergarten in the town of Minamisanriku. The plan was to rebuild the Asahi Kindergarten on higher ground, at a location owned by the Daioji Temple.

The temple was also home to a grove of huge cryptomeria (*sugi*) trees, which were killed by salt water flooding caused by the tsunami. Although the area was owned by the temple, the government still wanted to remove the trees and burn them for electricity generation. But we said "No, they belong to the local people, so we must use them to rebuild their town." This is how we decided to use the timber for the new kindergarten.

The trees were very tall—at least five meters in circumference and up to forty meters in height. Every piece of the building—from the structure to the handrails—was created from these trees, which had been planted after the tsunami in 1611, exactly 400 years earlier. But as natural materials they were not perfect. We had to do structural testing because there were weak spots and even animal nests in the wood. The columns are very heavy, 1.5 tons each, with a sectional dimension of 600 x 600 millimeters (2 x 2 feet). When you use this kind of tree, you have to make sure that each column is oriented to how it stood in the forest, because the tree bows in one direction and if you position it in a different way the wood could break apart. The widths of the planks also vary, because the trees are narrower at the top and thicker at the bottom.

The amazing thing is that all the carpenters in the area came to help put this

Sugi trees used in the construction of Asahi Kindergarten

Asahi Kindergarten

building up because they knew that this wood was made from trees that were a part of their local history. They were not interested in money; they wanted their pride and their history back. All other construction in the area stopped so that people could come to help build this project. Many villagers also came to the ceremony to put up the last

Ceremony for the installation of the last beam

beam. For some villagers, this was the first time they had smiled after the tsunami, after so many had lost their families.

It is important for the building to have long eaves because in summer it is very hot and in winter it is very cold, sometimes −15 degrees Celsius. Yet, the children use the space beneath the eaves to run and play.

Children in class and at play at Asahi Kindergarten

People always tell them, "You have to stand inside the handrails," but the children never do. This too is a part of their education. They also crawl underneath the floor, which is actually quite similar to a childhood memory I also have.

There is a famous monk at the temple who helped to save countless lives. He kept telling the local people, "If a tsunami happens, come to the temple on higher ground." The same monk is also the principal at the kindergarten. He looks so happy now, like an elementary school student himself!

But now the Japanese government is telling us that they are going to build a seawall along the coast. However, none of the locals want this because the sea is a part of their lives. The sea is at once a danger and also a treasure to them, and even where there were seawalls many people died because they could not see the water rising. Still the government does not understand alternatives to this strategy.

Instead of trying to stop the tsunami, we are trying to tell the story through architecture. If an earthquake happens, you have to come to this kindergarten for refuge, to the same trees killed by seawater on March 11, 2011. This is the statement I am trying to leave for the future. The project bears a message to those children who will likely encounter a tsunami in the next 400 years. The tsunami comes every 400 years; the last tsunami was in 1611, this time it was in 2011, and the next time it will be in 2411. We are quite sure of this.

A couple whose child had cancer came to us and asked us to create a humane space for children suffering

Concept diagram for the Child Chemo House

from cancer. In Japan, once a child is diagnosed with cancer they have to be kept in a quarantine zone at the hospital for six months because the chemicals kill white blood cells, suppressing their immune system. A mother naturally wants to stay with her child, but legally she is not supposed to stay at the hospital. What happens, then, is that the mother stays there for six months in the same room with her child. She must keep smiling, because when the mother smiles, the child also smiles. And although eighty percent of children survive treatment, one-third of families will have problems after the treatment because of the trauma

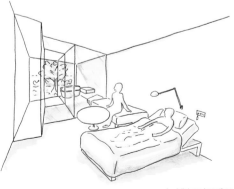

A child and mother

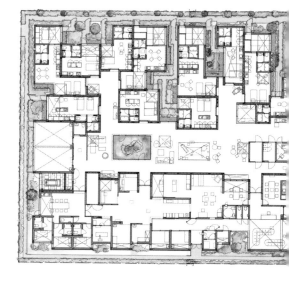

Plan of Child Chemo House

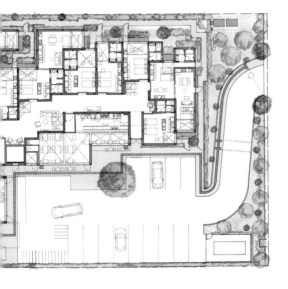

of such harsh conditions. So we tried to do something. We raised money for seven years, and now the Child Chemo House is built and will open in December 2013.

The concept started with us asking Japanese housing companies to donate houses to be located around the clinic. But we were told, "No, you can't do that because the children cannot walk outside." They suggested that we put the houses together like a village. And we thought, "Maybe it would be nice to have them together in small groups, because five people always work quite well as a group." Eventually, we came up with this type of clustered plan.

So now each patient has a room for their family. The patients can see their

Section sketch of Child Chemo House

parents and siblings, which reduced the quarantine period by two-thirds. Most of the time, the children can stay in the house zone, but when they are in very serious condition they can return to the space between the red and blue doors, to the clean room. So you use the two doors to control the degree of quarantine; and because we are not treating them in one big space, they have a much more humane life.

We have a problem as architects: our publications are only interested in the latest mode or style. But, the funny thing is that if you look at architecture magazines from ten years ago, most of the projects are now obsolete. We are supposed to design

品川501 と 58-32

The Tezukas in their Citroën 2CV

architecture to last at least fifty years, one hundred years, or sometimes even longer. We drive this car, the Citroën 2CV. It's not exactly efficient, but the amazing thing about the 2CV was that it was in production for fifty years. This car has one of the longest production runs in history, while Japanese car companies change their car designs as often as every year. I have tried to learn from this car. Of course there is no air conditioning, but the roof panel can be opened, which provides good ventilation. On rainy days we have to close the roof, but we have a small vent under the front windshield, which works extremely well, but, if you forget to close it before you get onto the expressway, all the water from the bonnet splashes into the interior and floods the floor! The instruction manual says there is a plug in the floor, and if you unplug it you can let all the water out! We can fit many things in this car, and many people, including our whole family.

The client of the Roof House once said, "You never get 100 percent satisfaction from Tezuka Architects. They are not perfect, but you love Tezuka architects 120 percent." That was the biggest compliment we've ever received. We are architects, but we are also human beings, and we cannot be perfect. But if you make something loved by people, architecture can survive. Architecture is not a thing, but an event. It is a living thing, a kind of symbiosis with human beings. We are not just one life form: from the microscopic life forms that help us live, to the buildings we live in, we are all connected. All we are trying to do is be a part of this symbiosis.

Thank you very much.

Student Question and Answer:

Takaharu Tezuka: Do you think we have time for questions? If you ask a good question, we have presents!

Mark Mulligan: But it must be a really good question....

TT: One book is from an architecture museum in Germany, from an exhibition we did in Frankfurt called *Nostalgic Future*, and these are our Japanese catalogues, so the three make one complete set.

Who wants to ask the first question? It must be a good question, right?

Student 1: My question is about color. You talked about color as it pertains to your family and how each of you is characterized by a different color, which you claim as a personal brand of sorts. But in your architecture, it actually doesn't seem to come into play at all. I was curious where that disjunction comes from? You are very playful in other respects—say with the form and your space making, but not with color necessarily. It's quite restrained actually.

TT: I think that is a very good question. For us, architecture is not the subject, as Mark said at the beginning. Originally, when we were asked to present our models and drawings at the Carnegie Museum, we told them no, because when we design architecture we are not trying to make objects. We are trying to see how people react in our architecture. It's abstract, I know, but do you understand what I mean?

So in the case of Fuji Kindergarten, children are the ones who bring the color. As you have seen in the slides I have shown tonight, you can see that it is the children who are very colorful. I think it's quite beautiful, actually. We collaborated with a graphic designer, Kashi Wasedo, and he designed the caps and uniforms. The children are the subjects and that is why we don't put color in our architecture. You know, if you put too many colors on a dish, beautiful cuisine cannot stand out. I am not saying we want to make a boring dish. Rather, I want to make a dish that makes the cuisine look better.

Student 2: I am wondering what's more important for you: narrative, form, material, or site? What comes first for you?

TT: Narrative or form? That's a very architectural question. As I said, architecture is a creature, so it cannot be solely site specific or entirely autonomous. Actually, that's something you taught me twenty-five years ago [points to Dean Mohsen Mostafavi]. Sometimes people ask me about the relationship between landscape and architecture. I say, there is no dominant or inferior thing, because everything is working in harmony.

In Christianity or in the Islamic world, there is one truth; but in Hinduism or in Japanese thinking there are many truths. When Jesus came to Japan we said, "Welcome to Japan! By the way, we have eight million gods waiting before you came. Please take a number and have a seat." So, when we consider architecture, we don't make autonomous objects or objects entirely incorporated into nature either. It doesn't stand alone, but at the same time it has its own existence, the same as Japanese architecture. Do you know the sketch by Jorn Utzon to describe Japanese architecture? It's just a sketch of a roof floating, but that simplicity between architecture and its surroundings is what I am talking about.

Student 3: Back home I was involved in many kindergarten projects, both in the design and also in the policy design of the building code. I got to a point where I was also sitting down with officials and designing how things should be built. One of the discussions we had was regarding your kindergarten. We presented it at one of our meetings, and the local officials didn't approve, saying that it could not be built. They claimed that the pedagogical model they desired could not be implemented in architecture such as this. They needed to have specific rooms being separated with specific doors, specific windows, et cetera.

I wanted to know if you used a specific pedagogical model to inform your design. How much does play within the children's education have to do with the end result of this project?

TT: We didn't resolve this ourselves. We could only do this because we had a client powerful enough to persuade his students and city hall. Actually, before this project, we had designed four kindergartens already, but he was the only one who fully understood our ideas. He was the only one powerful enough to push the idea through to the authorities.

It also doesn't just happen at once; it takes time to persuade people. You cannot always start by asking for approval. For example, in the hospital we designed, we couldn't get approval to make it a proper hospital, so we designed it as an apartment complex with a medical support system. Only after we built it did we take it to our government to get approval as a hospital. So, rethinking program is always a back-and-forth process. Sometimes, you have to find a way around. Of course, it also helps to have a really great client.

Student 4: I was wondering where or how did you develop such a sensibility for understanding architecture as a shelter to support human beings?

TT: As a way of answering your question, I'll tell you how I learned to understand children. First I found a girlfriend, then I got married, and then I had children of my own. Only then did I really get to know how they act. But that's how it works. You can only learn from experience, and the older you get, the more experiences you will have, and the more you will grow to understand other human beings.

Before this lecture, I was talking to a few students, and I was explaining how you can tell if a soup is tasty. If you ask a scientist to analyze why the soup is tasty, they will boil it to find the ingredients, but they won't be able to find the answer this way. But an old lady can tell you the answer! Imagine coming inside on a cold winter day, and your house is warm and your family is there waiting for you, and you sit down in front of a nice oak table, and she says, "I made this soup for you." These are the things that make the soup taste delicious.

It may seem simple, but that is architecture. When you practice science, you try to focus on one truth, but there is never just one truth, because architecture always exists in the balance between many factors. These days, students try to analyze everything too much. It is more important to observe things as they are and embrace the facts of the world.

Thank you all again for coming.

View to the courtyard at the Sora no Mori Clinic

More Blue than Before:
An Interview with
Takaharu Tezuka

Greg Logan

I first met Takaharu Tezuka in the summer of 2013 while working as an intern at his office in Tokyo. Unlike most design offices in the city, the Tezukas eschewed more trendy locales—like Omotesando or Roppongi—and instead elected to locate their office in the picturesque Todoroki Gorge at the edge of Setagaya Ward.

Although only there for a short while, I was struck by the warmth and humanity of the office. I worked the kind of reasonable schedule typically unheard of at a Japanese architecture firm, and evenings in the office were often broken up with communal dinners prepared in the office kitchen (it was tradition that departing employees cook the communal dinner on their last day of work and I was not exempt). It was a chaotic yet kind place to work, with boxes of models piled to the ceiling.

Since my departure, the office has expanded to the floor below, providing much-needed relief to the overflowing third floor. I met with Tezuka again in the autumn of 2015 to speak with him about his work, his inspiration, and the growth of his guiding philosophy. We met in the new, second-floor space, now dedicated to housing the office library, a few choice models, and a set of tables for meetings with clients. (While slightly less packed, the third floor was still reserved for the more messy day-to-day work of architecture.) It was late afternoon on a Saturday in November—autumn was beginning to transition to winter—and from the office's panoramic windows, I watched as twilight set in on the Todoroki Gorge.

Joining me were three members of Tezuka's staff: Midori Taki, Sockkee Ooi, and Aurapim Phongsirivech. As you will soon see, what started as a more formal interview quickly became a casual conversation among friends and colleagues. Familiarity always trumps formality in Tezuka's office.

Tezuka arrived to the interview with his hands bound in gauze. I assumed that he had somehow injured himself, perhaps while helping to build a model. Concerned, I asked Tezuka about his injuries, but he reassured me that he was, in fact, fine. He was merely running late and had come directly from his boxing workout without taking the time to unbind his hands. I've always been impressed with Tezuka's energy. Like a teenager, he will test his vertical leap by jumping up to touch a sign at a train station, and the office bike rides up Mt. Fuji are famously arduous (or infamous if one lacks the requisite cardiovascular health).

Once, while on the train back from Fuji Kindergarten, Tezuka pulled out a crisp new blue T-shirt from his bag, slipped it over his current one, and turned to me to ask for my opinion. I told him it looked fine. On hearing this, Tezuka pulled out his iPad from his bag and began tapping away at the device. After a minute or two he looked up and said to me, "I just bought twenty." This may seem odd or eccentric to the outsider, but to me this represents Tezuka: a man of limitless energy, curiosity, and commitment to his ideas.

This interview is about how Tezuka found his voice and how he continues to hone it. It is, in effect, about how he continues to become "bluer than before."

Greg Logan: It's a pleasure to see you again, Tezuka-san. As a jumping off point, I thought we might start with a discussion of the lecture you gave at Harvard a few years ago. The lecture dealt with your work in the abstract, your philosophies of design in application to specific projects. But, of course, at some point the philosophy needs to be translated into a physical building and must tackle technical and pragmatic concerns. I'm wondering how you bridge the gap between these two. How do you start with stories or philosophies and create something concrete, specific, and usable?

Takuharu Tezuka: In my opinion, human beings are part of a larger existence, but we often deny this situation. You know, in addition to our own human cells, we are also a collection of bacteria, but these days we are surrounded by antibacterial everything.

Recently, our office designed a hospital, Sora-no-mori, to treat women with fertility problems. Having a baby is a kind of natural cycle, a part of who we are. And we are not designed to procreate in a sterilized environment. The mother and the baby are both collections of microscopic life forms, and both are supposed to feel like a part of their surrounding environment. This is why we did not try to make a "hospital" for these women in the conventional sense. Instead, we tried to make something as close to the natural environment as possible.

Of course, when we deal with the ova we have to be very careful, because they are supposed to be inside the body of the mother, so when we remove the eggs for fertilization this has to be done with the utmost caution. However, if we are dealing with just the mother, we should treat her as a part of a natural ecosystem. Of course, we received a lot of complaints from the local government representing the Ministry of Health and Safety. They said that all hospitals have to be inside, and they thought that we exposed everything to the outside because we didn't have any money,

Model of the Sora no Mori Clinic

but this wasn't the case. We thought it would be better for the patients as human beings.

GL: So you're saying that we should start by really understanding human psychology and physiology and how space can make people happy, rather than setting out to make an iconic building that looks beautiful or interesting?

TT: Nowadays, we have fantastic computers, 3D printers, et cetera. We have the technology to do whatever we want. But there are much bigger issues that we haven't discussed as architects. These include asking what it means to be a human being. If you are talking with the principal of a kindergarten, they might ask you, "Is your architecture good for children?" If you start talking about geometry, they'll think you're crazy! It's not what they want. Of course, we can do whatever we want. We can make a building based on form. I'm not against these, but there are more important things that we have to fight for almost every day. These days, we are not really fighting for

design. Mostly, we are fighting to understand other people. That is very important to
us. My point is that it is very important to deal
with people as a part of a larger existence.
That is how we design things. Architecture
is the thing that relates humans to their
environment. In short, our theory is one of
expansion rather than contraction. Instead
of going inward we try to expand the story.

GL: I am very interested in the way you
talk about bacteria. It feels extremely
expressive and dynamic. It reminds me of
Kenzo Tange's theory of Jomon and Yayoi.[1]
It feels very Jomon to me, very primitive.
For example, in your project in Niigata I see
something very primitive. But then again
many of your buildings can be quite clean
and precise.

TT: Well, sometimes I have to be Yayoi.

---

1. The modernist architect Kenzo Tange theorized that the height
of Japanese architecture occurred when two aesthetic modes
(embodied in two Japanese prehistoric eras) were in harmony.
The Jomon Period, or Japan's prehistoric hunter-gatherer
period, embodied the dynamic and visceral. The Yayoi Period, in
contrast, with the advent of agriculture and raised grain storage,
represented the rational and logical.

GL: You wrote a book called *Nostalgic Future.* Of course, you're being playful here; nostalgia is about looking backward, but the future is all about looking forward. But I'm wondering how you reconcile the two. Do you see yourself as nostalgic, a futurist, or both? I know drawing is very important to you, but at the same time you draw on an iPad. Is hand drawing a nostalgic act or is drawing on an iPad a futuristic one? I'm wondering how you feel about the past and the future and how this dialogue manifests itself in your work.

TT: I think a title like "Nostalgic Future" is meant to contain a bit of irony. But I do believe that sometimes there is no difference between past, present, and future. People have been living on the earth with architecture for a long time. The history of architecture is as long as the history of humans, and there are those who say that before we started making architecture we were simply apes.

These days we are always talking about what is coming next month or next year. What did Rem Koolhaas say? What is MVRDV doing? Or BIG? Or Junya Ishigami? But it's irrelevant, it has no meaning for me. We are designing things for the next fifty years, the next one hundred years. If you think about what people were doing fifty years ago, there was no way to predict how we live now. You know the movie *Modern Times*? Its director, Charlie Chaplin, had a vision of the future where we were going to live in a machine age controlled by huge steam engines. But it didn't happen. You don't see any huge gears around now, or cars flying overhead. When the computer came out, movie directors thought the future would be one dominated by the computer and many shifted their visions to a future based on computer-aided design. However, this is not really a true step forward. It's very important to understand that the future is not a place that we don't know. It is within us.

GL: Still, it's fun to imagine the future. And I hear that you are a big *Star Trek* fan, correct?

TT: Yes, I am!

GL: On its surface, of course, it is very future oriented, but there are universal themes of humanity, exploration, and understanding embedded in the series. I'm wondering if you pull any particular lessons from it.

TT: Well, I was not prepared for this [laughs]. First of all, the most amazing idea I have found in *Star Trek* is the holodeck. You can create whatever kind of environment you'd like in the room. It's very different from Disneyland. Disneyland is just an attraction while the holodeck is much more interactive. That is a very interesting concept to me: to understand the future and the past existing at the same time, and the idea that human beings are essentially the same at all times.

GL: I hear a certain amount of ambivalence about science from you. In the lecture, you talk about soup and how you can't understand its taste strictly through science. Its taste is a feeling based on context. But at the same time, you talk about rational design that's based on science. For example, you mentioned sound engineering from Indonesia based on a certain understanding of human physiology. Obviously science has a role—we couldn't be a modern society without it—but I like what you said earlier, "human beings are the constant." I'm wondering if that's what you keep coming back to. Is the bottom line for you human well-being?

TT: Exactly.

GL: For that reason, I believe you could say that the Tezuka design process starts with the very specific well-being of your client. Your projects often seem to start with a meeting with your client in which you come up with an innovative or ambitious design plan—like living on the roof or having an outdoor clinic—but then you have some sort of difficult discussion with authorities where you have to convince them that it can work.

TT: Well, it's not a confrontation. I prefer to have a drink and talk with them [laughs].

GL: I'm wondering if this is an inevitability of ambitious program design. Does innovation take a certain amount of convincing because it is outside what is considered "normal"? Is the fact that you are able to get so many projects like this built a testament to having very understanding clients, or perhaps to you being very charming and persuasive with government officials?

TT: I would say that I don't persuade people to see things my way. Rather, it's a kind of optimization. We start our projects by meeting with the client. Sometimes we survive the meeting process and sometimes we don't. But meeting with many people in general is very important for me. Some people ask, "Why do you give so many lectures?" I don't decline lectures so easily, but it's not because I need to tell my story to others. When I go to lectures in places like the Middle East or South America, I meet people I have never seen in Japan. They have quite a different way of thinking and I get something from that. From this, I can find different ideas that I can combine in many different ways. That's how it works. You can find interesting people anywhere, and there are so many of them. I have also found that most people in this world are quite reasonable. There are few people who don't understand what I am talking about.

Of course, there are always loud minorities. There are a lot of people making knee-jerk, politically correct statements these days. For example, people say we should put vegetation on top of our architecture, but of course, environmental and economic systems are more complicated than that. But people think, "Oh, that's green and it looks so environmentally friendly." I think we need to be very careful when we talk about the environment.

People say, "Of course LEDs are good," but recently some newspapers or government officials are saying we should completely eradicate incandescents. We professionals need to say that this is wrong. There are no absolute answers. Of course, some government or local authorities are affected by a small number of vocal people, but they remain the minority. I think my role is to think as most people think and feel as most people feel.

GL: What I'm hearing is that it's dangerous to overgeneralize. To use one of your built works as an example, it would be easy to overgeneralize and say people shouldn't be living on their roofs, yes?

TT: Yeah. I think it's true. I think it's very important to accept diversity. If you don't accept these differences you are going to deny the meaning and complexity of culture.

Midori Taki: So you're going back and back to the root of ideas? You said that you test your ideas or get different values when meeting new people, but I think you're also saying that you take different values from different worlds. So it's like you have different drawers to pull from, and when you talk with a client you are able to choose a specific drawer for the situation. I think you really have a vast knowledge of architecture. That's what I have realized working for you.

TT: Working *with* me.

MT: So yeah, it really makes sense. You won't really see it at first. It takes a bit of time to see the depth of his knowledge. I always wonder how many drawers he has [laughs].

GL: That raises an interesting question regarding style. You say you're very interested in diversity, but you seem to come back to certain forms or materials quite often: I see a lot of buildings that are circles or ovals, you like timber quite a bit, you often work with similar programs (schools, et cetera).

TT: You know, when we give a lecture outside Japan some people ask me, "How can I be international?" or, "How can I be famous?" I'm not sure if I'm famous enough to answer these questions, but I know that finding yourself is the key, because everyone is unique. You are different even from your twin brother because he has different experiences than you. There is nobody like you. Maybe there are some who are similar, but you are quite unique. Understanding what makes you unique leads your architecture to also be unique. If someone comes to you with a project, they don't want the same thing they can find somewhere else. They want you. So I suppose I am doing the same thing. It's strange, but as I continue to understand the diversity of others, I can be more and more myself.

GL: So, you have become increasingly confident with yourself?

TT: It's not about confidence but about reaching a better understanding of myself. Feeling confident implies superiority to others. What I am saying is that I am becoming bluer than before [laughs].

GL: You know, one of the things I think about when I think of a "Tezuka style" is a certain amount of simplicity. I remember working on a detail for the Sora-no-mori project and I had a few models prepared, and you took one that I thought was already simple enough and starting pulling pieces off it, saying, "It's too complicated!" Furthermore, I think there is a difference between simplicity and minimalism. Minimalism is an aesthetic mode that can often belie a certain messiness below the surface. Simplicity, on the other hand, is an approach based on process that permeates aesthetics and construction. I'm wondering why simplicity is so important to you.

TT: Well, it's not simplicity for simplicity's sake. Rather, it's a kind of obsession.

GL: Obsession with?

TT: People say I am very persistent in what I do. I never stop. For example, once I start playing piano I'll keep playing for days. When I was a kid my mother had to stop me, because I could play from eight in the morning until midnight only stopping to eat occasionally. But that is who I am. When I start designing things, I try to understand what it is, right? What I'm saying is that what we are doing is not truly simple. Everything in this world has so much depth. You know, the movie *The Powers of Ten* by Charles and Ray Eames? They start from the scale of the human, then zoom out to that of the universe, and finally back into the scales of cells and atoms. The level of architecture is somewhere in the middle. There are so many things you can see at this scale. So in order to experience this depth of scale, you have to really get close to the work, right? And I think that causes our architecture to seem really simple, but it is not simple at all.

GL: It seems as if your focus leads you to a very solitary goal. And because of that, there is a oneness or coherency in the narrative of your work as opposed to something that might be overly complex or busy. Is that fair?

TT: You know, there are people who tell me that I am like a single-cell organism. A fellow architect told me once that he didn't understand the design of the Roof House because if you want to be outside, why not just sit in a field? But I told him that the

design of the Roof House is about more
than just sitting on the roof. First, you need
to know the best inclination for sitting down.
Next, you have to have walls of a certain
height to have the right amount of privacy.
Then you need to have a table, otherwise
you won't be able to have a party on top of
the roof. And you have to have a kitchen, a
washbasin, a way to get up to the roof, and
maybe you want to have a shower up there
for summertime. You have to have the right
type of timber on top of the roof. If you have
a metal roof it will be too hot to sit on. It looks
like just one interesting idea, but it raises so
many things you can talk and talk about. So
it's not simple at all. In the end, I am not a
single-cell organism.

GL: That's exactly what I was talking about
in the beginning. It's also what we have been
dancing around this entire time: the idea of
human-centered design. Using the Roof
House as an example, you start to show how
human-centered design leads to some very
specific decisions: the pitch of the roof, the

materials used, what is needed to realize a domestic life on top of the house, et cetera.

TT: I think you need to know that diversity needs specificity sometimes. When we design something, we can't be neutral. The things you can do with one piece of architecture are very limited, so if you are designing just one thing, that thing should have color. If you make everything in neutral gray, the whole picture becomes gray. Like the paintings of Seurat, each dot needs its own beautiful color; each dot should be very specific. Only then can you begin to make out the whole. That is the city. As an architect, I am trying to be very specific.

But when I talk about the city I have a different attitude. I say, don't go for the specific. Rather, we should allow for the diversity of activities that people are capable of in the city. Currently, we are designing a high-rise in Shibuya, but for this project I am trying not to think like an architect. Rather, I want to be a city planner, because there are going to be a huge number of people working there. Possibly more than 100,000 people will be going in and out of that building every day. Every day! So I don't want to control the design too much. I'm happy to have one of those restaurants with the big moving crabs outside. I don't hate that. That kind of diversity is the city. So, when we design big things I don't want to control everything.

I learned this approach from Yasuhiro Hamano. He's a very interesting person. He was one of my mentors and he also gave me one of my first projects. He is a very important figure as a city planner. You know Takeshita-Dori or Cat Street in Harajuku, right? He was the creator of both. He also has a strong presence in the fashion industry. He does so many things. But ultimately, he is an organizer; he has a passion for what humans and the city are supposed to be, and he taught to us about the importance of diversity in the city. He always told us that it's wrong to have just one architect design an entire street or block.

GL: Right. That's why corporate campuses or master plans designed by one person are always so dead and lifeless.

TT: Exactly. So, coming back to our previous discussion: why do you want the specific? It's a matter of scale, you know? If you were designing just one house, it has to be very specific, very small, because you are designing things for specific people. But if you are designing for maybe 3,000 people, it becomes a little more complex because you have to respond to complex needs. And if you are designing a building like the one we are working on in Shibuya—with more than 100,000 people coming through every day—then you have to design for that level of diversity. So, how you stand back from the picture is what matters.

GL: I'm wondering how this process works. How do you take these larger issues and implement them in the office? How do you start to take those ideas and make them more, for lack of a better word, architectural?

We've discussed how you start with the human as a constant, but what comes next?

TT: I think the key is education—because I can't do everything myself. Of course, I *try* to design everything, but it's impossible. However, I also don't want to be so busy that I have a project I've never had time to visit myself. Therefore, I need to educate the people around me. That is why I don't stop teaching. You know, the money I'm earning as a professor is too little. The amount I get in a month can be spent in my office in a half day. It's not financially good for my office, but it is very important for me because it means that there are more and more people who understand my way of thinking. In my office I try to talk to young architects as much as possible. Of course, I never have enough time, but there are always a certain few who start to understand. You know, Midori has been in my office for quite a long time. It takes a long time to develop educated people, but once they reach a certain stage wonderful and unexpected things start emerging from them.

When I started my office I decided not to work by myself. From the beginning I worked with my wife, Yui, so that we could share ideas. And when we got our first project, I tried to hire people, but at the time I didn't have enough money so I had to split it between people. Do you know TNA (Nabeshima and Takei)? The amount they

Takaharu and Yui with Richard Rogers

got was exactly the same as what Yui and I got. Of course, we could have done the project by ourselves, but we thought that if it were just the two of us we wouldn't be able go beyond our own expectations. As I said, architecture cannot be done by one person, and I have always been inspired by my experiences with other people, including those in my office.

Education is a very important part of my life and I learned that from Richard Rogers. You know Richard Rogers isn't the best draftsman, but he is a very good thinker and he's very good at talking to people. One day when we were working on a competition, he brought a tray of ice cream to the table. He brought ice cream for everyone! And when he brought some to me I was so impressed. He also used to go out for dinner with just the young architects in the office, so that he could have a chance to talk with them one-on-one. These experiences were really important to me. I was able to understand what kind of person he was, and I now try to do the same for those in my office. I wanted to stay there much longer, but I had to return to Japan because of a green card problem. I was there for only four years, but I believe that what I got from Richard Rogers and Partners will stay with me for the rest of my life. I still feel that Richard Rogers and Partners is my home.

GL: You mentioned your wife, Yui. I'm wondering how the division of work happens between the two of you. I know you collaborate with her during the design process, but how does this work? Do you sit down and make decisions together?

TT: Actually, she is the better side of my heart. Do you know what I mean? It's very difficult to explain, but when I design, I need to be careful that my personality doesn't get the better of me. I'm always at risk of doing selfish design. I am very good at making models and drawings, at doing things very quickly. I have always been a very fast designer, but this approach leads to so many bad decisions, and in the end, even though it might look good, I know it was the wrong thing to do. But Yui is very good at finding the moral center to a design. I always try to get her opinion on a design. Yesterday, I showed her a model and said, "It's a fantastic design."

And she said, "Well, it's not so bad, but I think you should raise the building a bit more."

"But the model is all glued!" I said.

She said, "No, no, you have to do something." So she grabbed a knife. Then she said, "There's something wrong with the gutter."

I said, "Don't worry," and I cut it off and said, "How about now?"

She said, "Well … now it's not so bad. Now it's okay." That is how it works.

GL: That's a great example. We've talked a lot about family. I'm interested in your thoughts on family. I know your father was an architect.

TT: Yes. He was an architect working for a large company. Actually he applied to work for Oscar Niemeyer, but ultimately wasn't able to go due to family reasons. As a young architect, he was the chief architect of a joint venture working on the Imperial Palace with the architect Junzo Yoshimura. At the time, Yoshimura's office was even smaller than my office is now, so the government wanted a large organization to help. They asked a few companies to put together a design team, and my father was the head of the team, so he was communicating with Yoshimura all the time.

GL: When you were growing up was there a lot of play or other creative activities in the household?

Takaharu with his father

TT: First of all, the house in which I grew up was designed by my father. It looked just like a Junzo Yoshimura design. It wasn't as sophisticated as a Yoshimura design, but it was good enough for me [laughs]. Secondly, there were always so many architecture magazines around the house. At the time, he was working on one of the foundational architectural journals in Japan, *Space Design* (SD). In fact, I still have the first issue of *SD* in my house. There were also lots of architecture models around the house. Once he finished a project, instead of throwing a model away he would bring it home and I would play with it. Also, there was a book of architectural drawings for the imperial palace, and I would often look through it to try to understand the design. Even though I was in elementary school, I knew how many stairs there were to the second floor, the name of each room, and the design of lanterns and wall finishes. It was quite unusual for a child.

However, I must say that I wasn't a great student at the time. I wasn't so bad, just a normal student at a public elementary school. But in junior high school I got a recommendation for the high school for Tokyo City University. I didn't need to take any exams to get in, so everything was very relaxed. It was at this time that I started studying in the architecture department, but I found that I was very different from my peers, so a professor of mine said I should leave Japan and go abroad. That is why I applied to the Ivy League schools. I applied to the University of Pennsylvania, Harvard, Princeton, and MIT; Harvard was the only one that didn't accept me [laughs]. Maybe my GRE wasn't good enough. In any case, that year I received a scholarship from Penn, and it was also a very good year for the school, so I decided to go there. That is how it started. All of this was the result of the environment that my father created. He never forced me to be an architect. He never told me to be an architect. He just told me that it was not an easy job.

GL: You spent quite a bit of time abroad studying at Penn and working for Richard Rogers, but eventually you came back here to Japan. How do you think your design experiences abroad complement those learned in Japan?

TT: You know, I can never stop being Japanese, but when we started the office I never felt that we were doing Japanese design. I first realized I was doing Japanese design when an Italian journalist came to Japan. He was writing about the Engawa House. He said, "Oh, you are really Japanese." And even as he was saying this I was saying to myself, "Oh, maybe I am Japanese." But, of course, it is a part of my genes; it's how I grew up. But maybe I am not the same type of Japanese as most people living in Tokyo.

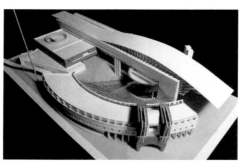

Model of studio project at the University of Pennsylvania

GL: Because of your experiences abroad?

TT: Yeah, but also because I have a connection to Saga prefecture. My grandfather's house connects to the environment in a very interesting way. All of these things are a part of me. It makes me unique. Also, as I said, my father exposed me to so many things at an early age. So I think that all of this made me very different from others, but still Japanese. I am proud that my work looks Japanese.

GL: What does that mean to you? Is it a style? It is a sensibility? Is it an attention to climate and material? Is it all of these things?

Hand rendering of studio project at the University of Pennsylvania

TT: Maybe your question is the same as asking, "What part of your face is Japanese?" It's a balance between eyes, mouth, and nose. It's impossible to say where the Japanese is, but maybe the answer lies somewhere a bit deeper.

MT: I have a question. From my experience working with you and reading interviews you have done or books you have written, you have a very clear philosophy and unique approach to architecture. Now that you have reached a certain age and your office has reached a certain level of success, I wouldn't call you a young architect anymore [everyone laughs]. I mean that in a good way! You are established. You have risen to another age group of architects, but I want to know if the establishment of your philosophy came from a very young age. I mean at twenty or thirty did you have these ideas, or did they come from twenty years of collecting and lecturing and meeting people? How did you develop this philosophy?

TT: I'm not sure if I was as thoughtful as you are, Midori. When I was your age, I was really struggling with a philosophy at that time. So I would say that twenty years ago I was a different person than I am now, and that I am going to be yet another person in ten years. I have heard from many people that Fumihiko Maki was quite charismatic as a young man; but now he has such a quiet dignity. I hope to be like Maki-san one day. That would be great! [laughs]. But my personality has never changed. In a few weeks, I will go to an end of the year party (*bounenkai*) with my colleagues from elementary school. Every year they tell me, "You have been the same since you were six years old. You never change!" That is just my personality. However, my philosophy has changed. That's because if a chance presents itself I will jump on it. With even just the slightest chance of success I will make the leap while others might hesitate, because even when I fail to get a project I learn something. The most important thing is to always remain positive. Your philosophy will develop in time.

Sockkee Ooi: It seems like you always say that developing a philosophy takes time and that you can only come to this through age. I'm wondering what hope there is for me now [laughs].

TT: No, no. You can always speed this up.

SO: Another way of saying this is: what were you doing when you were my age?

TT: I was finding my girlfriend [laughs]. I got married so quickly. At twenty-five I was just about to leave UPenn to move to London. I was having all kinds of fun.

MT: I think I can explain a bit. It's all about trying to see what others are thinking or what they care about. I think that is what Tezuka-san is saying when he talks about accumulating experiences. It doesn't really have to be a boyfriend or girlfriend, just someone you can share a moment with.

GL: Right, the more relationships you build the more empathy you build.

TT: Yeah, it's true. Until I met Yui I was always just thinking about myself. I was thinking only about my needs and what I wanted to become. But when I am with Yui, I have to make sure I know where she is.

SO: Maybe Yui-san would like to hear this! [laughs].

TT: Well she gets lost all the time.

MT: Yeah! It just happened very recently. When we were going to a meeting the other day, she began to walk away on a different path. Tezuka-san grabbed her coat and said, "Not that way!" And she was just laughing saying, "oh!"

TT: Yeah, but it has been fun. It has made me a different person. She has broadened my view.

MT: One more question. Maybe it was a bit different when you were a young architect, but nowadays we are constantly flooded with media and information and books and interviews and theories about so many people's work, and young architects like me become overwhelmed with finding our own path. The field has become so complicated and difficult. What advice would you give to people like me or your students on how to find themselves in such a complex world flooded with information?

TT: Actually, that isn't just a contemporary problem: when we started the office twenty years ago, students weren't so different from the ones now. But for me, there was one architect who always kept me focused and standing tall. His name is Teichi Takahashi. He was a very good architect! He was especially good with concrete. Actually, Yui's father was the first employee in his office.

　　Since that time, we have been close with Takahashi-san. When we got married he came to our wedding party. He was like the best man, and since that time he has considered himself the godfather of Tezuka Architects. He always told us, "It doesn't matter what you publish as long as you are making good projects. As long as you're doing that, you'll be okay. You need to make sure you are proud of your projects. That's all that matters. Don't worry about publications."

You know, it's true. When you do good projects, people will come to understand your work and recognition will often follow. For example, we don't actually apply to many competitions. My office is very different in this respect. Rather, we focus our efforts on the small number of commissions we have at any given time. Even small ones get our full attention. You can start from a toilet, but as long as it is well done you will be given another chance. You don't need to be distracted by magazines or the Internet. The only thing that matters is to continue doing really good work.

GL: To that end, I'm wondering if you have any advice for young architects on building their intuition. Part of an architect's job is to understand a situation and make decisions quickly. But you never have time to take it all in; you have to feel the information intuitively.

How do we learn to make decisions faster and to trust those decisions?

Aurapim Phongsirivech: It's like the book *Thinking Fast and Slow*. Do you know it? It talks about two patterns of thinking: thinking slowly, which is the analytical taking in of information or incorporating past experiences in order to make decisions, and thinking fast, which is something more intuitive. Therefore, full decisions are half from experience and half from something more primitive. Is that what you mean?

GL: Yeah. Of course you can't get to this point without a certain amount of work. You have to have learned it and pulled it into your body, but when you are asked to do it you don't have to explain all the practicing that went into it. You just do it.

TT: Well, decision-making is different from intuition. Decisions are based on algorithms you construct for yourself, how you analyze a situation from your knowledge and experience. But no matter how much experience you have, you always want to get there faster. Intuition is something different, however. Something deep in your mind is telling you which way to go. But if a student of mine makes an intuitive judgment, I always challenge them to find the reason why they chose they way they did. Causality is a very important process, but ultimately these are two kinds of thinking that are in balance. That is what we are as thinking people. Many people think that I am intuitive, that I come up with ideas very quickly, but it's not true. Rather, many things come out of the slow process of building experiences. Actually, I would say Yui is much more intuitive than I am.

MT: I think you're right!

TT: I write many things down and I am always drawing. From these options, I try to find similar kinds of answers, and when I find an answer, sometimes it fits my expectations, but unexpected answers sometimes emerge. It's like the roof on the house the other day. Yui came to the office and she got the knife and turned it 180 degrees and suddenly the exterior became very different. That is quite an intuitive action. But you must remember that you can't change who you are. I have always been like this and until I go to my grave I am going to be like this. So when you ask me "how I can be intuitive?" well, in order to answer this maybe I would have to do it all over again.

MT: Coming back to the lecture for a moment, you always talk about stories. Why is that? What do you try to tell the students through this approach?

TT: If you speak only in abstract concepts, you can only communicate with a very specific group of people. But if you can tell a story, you can visualize ideas, which makes them universal. People have always been storytellers. I wish there was a better way to convey ideas, but I have always found stories work best. Maybe that is what I am, in the end, a storyteller. It's funny, my son is also a very good storyteller.

GL: Certainly that is the structure of the lecture. It's a series of stories about different projects. As a way to start wrapping things up, I'm curious how you see yourself moving forward. Do you have specific goals or are you just focused on one project at a time? Are there different types of research investigations you'd like to do? What is the future of Tezuka Architects, or are you not concerned with that? Are you just concerned with the present and the projects at hand?

TT: I want to design something that will stand for 400 years. That is what I have been saying lately.

GL: In Japan, that can be tough, though.

TT: That doesn't matter. Maybe you know the project in Minami Sanriku. We designed the project to stand for 400 years because the last tsunami came in 1611 and this time it came in 2011, 400 years later. In 1611, people had no idea what architecture would look like in 400 years. That's what makes it a really difficult goal, but one that I wish to pursue. What we can achieve within a lifetime is very small. Maybe the biggest achievement we can make is raising our children because children are going to have children of their own, and that eventually builds a society. Even architecture that has become famous in a publication or on the Internet might not stand for even twenty or thirty years. But if you look at Notre Dame, even the name of the architect is not there. The architecture is merely a servant to the people inside it. I want to do something that is going to serve the human race for a long time. Maybe I'm asking for something impossible. To date I've designed over 150 buildings. Maybe I'm hoping that just one or two survive for 400 years. That is what I'm hoping for. You know, one way of achieving this is by making architecture that will last for the next 400 years. The other way is to leave some kind of idea for the future. As I said, being a professor is important for me because I am leaving something for the minds of my students. I am sure I have taught some people who are now quite different from when they first met me. Maybe it's a

different answer from the one you expected,
but this is the only way I can say it.

The Daioji monk at Asahi Kindergarten

Reflections

Thomas Sherman

In the spring of 2015, through a Frederick Sheldon Traveling Fellowship awarded by Harvard University, I was fortunate enough to spend two months in Japan for research on contemporary timber architecture, tracing the relationship of wood buildings to sustainable forestry and fabrication processes. In reviewing potential case studies that would align with this research, I focused on the Asahi Kindergarten project, built in 2012 by Tezuka Architects. Delving into this project rekindled memories of Takaharu Tezuka's lecture "Beyond Architecture" at Harvard Graduate School of Design (GSD), which was the first time I had ever heard the story of the massive *sugi* trees used to build the kindergarten. Tezuka Architects had artfully designed the building with deliberate connections to the cultural and environmental context of post-tsunami Minamisanriku.

Eager to find a way to visit the Asahi Kindergarten, I reached out to Tezuka Architects through Greg Logan, a GSD colleague who had interned at the studio. Initial discussions with the staff at Tezuka Architects revealed that it was going to be difficult to organize a trip because the school was now located in the midst of an extensive land clearing and leveling project to create a new elevated site for the town of Minamisanriku. This earthwork had necessitated the temporary closing of the kindergarten, and access to the building was restricted. Even four years after the tsunami, the town still had limited train and road access, and the entire commercial district and fishing port had yet to be rebuilt.

After numerous discussions, Takaharu Tezuka graciously invited me to accompany their design team on a trip north to the Asahi Kindergarten on March 20,

2015 for a meeting regarding an addition to the school. Joining their group early in the morning at the Sendai train station, I hitched a ride with the team for a two-hour drive by van through Miyagi Prefecture to Minamisanriku. It was a unique opportunity to visit the school and to meet a monk from Daioji Temple (a Buddhist temple in Minamisanriku), who was instrumental in the planning of the new kindergarten. Expanding on this experience, this essay highlights a series of conversations from that day.

There had been 3,000 people living in Minamisanriku before the tsunami hit on March 11, 2011, and four years later only around 1,000 remained in the town. Some residents were killed in the disaster, but many lost everything and had to relocate to other areas across Japan. The monk from Daioji Temple stated, "It is so important to be acquainted with your neighbors. When you lose these neighbors, life changes so much." He expressed how even though many residents were able to find temporary housing, those who were relocated struggled the most without the neighborly support network they had developed in Minamisanriku.

In the aftermath of disasters like the 2011 Tohoku earthquake and tsunami, it is common to suggest temporary reconstruction projects and provisional buildings. In contrast, Takaharu Tezuka emphasized the social value and reinvestment in human dignity that longer term, more permanent reconstruction brings. The Asahi Kindergarten elevated this issue, as it was planned and funded shortly after the tsunami and could have shifted into the category of temporary project. Resisting this tendency, Takaharu Tezuka pushed for a design and material language in timber more intrinsically related to the local culture, one that alluded directly to the cyclical history of the tsunami in the region.

Tezuka Architects did not aim to deny the history of the tsunami in Miyagi Prefecture, but to emphasize the resourcefulness of the local inhabitants who have learned to live through these cyclical events of devastation. Tezuka notes, "Instead of stopping the tsunami, we tried to tell a story through architecture." Understanding that the history of multiple tsunami events is manifest in the Asahi Kindergarten, it provided the local residents a way of tracing their relationship to the region and their ancestors. Because UNICEF had initially asked Tezuka Architects to design a temporary school, the Asahi Kindergarten presented a unique model for the question of permanence. As expressed by Tezuka, "the money invested in a temporary structure would have been a waste in the long term." Similarly, the monk at Daioji Temple pushed for the new kindergarten to be considered a permanent structure, sensing the long-term needs of the local children. Immediately after the tsunami, the kindergarten temporarily occupied a local community building, which had traditional sliding panels and tatami mat floors. Tezuka found that this space worked well for the children, despite not meeting the government's planning requirements for school design. The sliding *shoji* screens were the only interior separation, and he wanted to carry the essence of this concept into the new building.

Influenced by historical Japanese timber construction, the design of the kindergarten's through-tenon joinery relied on wood wedges rather than metal connectors, which took advantage of the opportunity afforded by the massive local sugi trees. Because many of the regional carpentry shops had been destroyed by the tsunami, the milling, air-drying, and timber prefabrication was done by the Chuto company outside of Miyagi Prefecture. Relying on traditional knowledge, the cores of the huge timber columns (600 x 600 millimeters) were bored out with specialty equipment to help control checking and drying. The final on-site assembly of the timber frame directly involved local *daiku* (carpenters) who proudly came together to raise the building.

Tezuka envisioned the Asahi Kindergarten as a 400-year building—one that will be there as a reminder to future generations. He told me, "Architecture should support society, but should also extend its era." Furthermore, he suggested that many contemporary architects have succumbed to a sense of disposability, which allows design freedom but reinforces wastefulness. In contrast, he noted the example of his grandfather's house, which is more than one hundred years old: "It is wrong to say that Japanese culture is about disposability. In Japan all the oldest buildings are built of wood, and individual pieces can be replaced." For example, Horyuji Temple and its five-level pagoda near Nara have survived 1,200 years, but have had many of the timber components replaced through the years. Similarly, Tezuka notes the constant regeneration of the human body, where cells are continuously replaced over time. As long as a building's structure is reasonably strong, it can last for generations. Tezuka accepts change in his buildings over time; he does not fight this reality. Instead, he told me, "people's lifestyles are constantly changing, but if you can replace some parts, or make an extension—like the old cathedrals in Europe that have been changed over time—a building can last. I don't mind if someone adds layers to my buildings. It's not a sculpture, or a monument; it's alive. I want people to use my buildings and add to them."

In contrast to this way of thinking, the nationally funded reconstruction efforts have planned the new city of Minamisanriku thirty meters above sea level, on a new site further inland from the original town. These policies are a contentious subject, and Takaharu Tezuka expressed disagreement with the earthwork that has reduced the mountains to provide fill to raise the town. Immediately after the tsunami, the government settled on contracts for reconstruction, but didn't necessarily take into consideration the opinions of the local residents.

Tezuka Architect's design for the Asahi Kindergarten initiated a dialogue with the people of Minamisanriku. The construction of the kindergarten gave residents a reason to smile, they felt appreciated, and the process helped to heal deeper, less visible wounds. While it may have been easier to bring in trailer classroom units built of plywood and laminates, this solution would never have made the children or their parents feel dignified. Building the school from trees that their ancestors had planted allowed them some reconciliation to a history that had nearly been washed away. The architecture of the kindergarten not only embodies the history of the town in its *sugi* timber framing, but it also acts as an armature for the future, a future that acknowledges both the power of the tsunami and the strength of the people of Miyagi Prefecture. This symbiosis with the user and the site grounds the structure within the cultural, historical, and environmental network of its context, setting up feedback with a greater ecological sensibility. I left with an appreciation for Tezuka Architects' ability to directly connect to those who use and rely on their buildings, and for their capacity to project these values to an increasingly diverse and more global audience.

About the Editors

Thomas Sherman completed a Master of Design Studies (MDes) with a concentration in Energy and Environments at the Harvard Graduate School of Design (GSD) in 2014. Following graduation, Tom embarked on a Frederick Sheldon Traveling Fellowship for research on contemporary mass-timber architecture across Europe, Japan, and Canada. This research brought Tom to Tezuka Architects in the spring of 2015, with visits to a number of the studio's projects. While a student at the GSD, Tom and several colleagues won the 3rd LIXIL Architectural Competition for the design of Horizon House, an eighty-square-meter, low-energy, timber house in Taiki-cho, Hokkaido, Japan (published in the design magazine a+u 2013:06). This collaborative project provided an opportunity to work in Tokyo during the summer of 2013, and initiated a continuing interest in Japanese architecture and craft.

Greg Logan is a Masters in Architecture (MArch I) candidate at the Harvard Graduate School of Design, who worked at Tezuka Architects in the summer of 2013. During his time at Harvard, Greg has been a teaching fellow for Yukio Lippit's course on Japanese architecture, as well as a graphic designer and translator for the exhibit "The Thinking Hand: Tools and Traditions of the Japanese Carpenter." Greg's most recent sojourn to Japan was spent working for the firm of Maki and Associates and conducting research on seasonality in Japanese architecture, and was sponsored by a grant from Harvard's Reischauer Institute of Japanese Studies. Before studying at Harvard, Greg earned a Master's degree in Japanese Studies from Sophia University in Tokyo where he studied as a recipient of the Monbukagakusho scholarship.